I0520847

Fortune Written on Wet Grass

by
Eileen Murphy

The Wapshott Press

Fortune Written on Wet Grass, by Eileen Murphy, copyright 2019, and is reprinted here with the copyright owner's permission. Poetrylandia, Issue 3, The Wapshott Journal of Poetry, ISSN 2688-853X, ISBN 978-1-942007-31-9 is published at intervals by the Wapshott Press, now a 501(c)(3) nonprofit, PO Box 31513, Los Angeles, California, 90031-0513, telephone 323-201-7147. All correspondence can be sent to The Wapshott Press, PO Box 31513, LA CA 90031-0513. Visit our website at www.WapshottPress.org to learn more. This work is copyright © 2020 by Poetrylandia, founded 2019, edited by Ginger Mayerson.

Poetrylandia is always seeking quality poetry in any format. Please have a look at our submission guidelines at www.WapshottPress.org/Poetrylandia or email the editor at editor@wapshottpress.org

Donations happily accepted at donate.wapshottpress.org

Cover design: Mish

Fortune Written on Wet Grass

by Eileen Murphy

Contents

Fortune Written on Wet Grass

by
Eileen Murphy

Fortune Written on Wet Grass

All over Florida,

it's drizzling

with dazzling monotony.
The rain is warm
as a baby's breath

and a sweat drop drools

down the middle

of my shirt

and cradles

itself in my cleavage

and I hear

the rain

talking to me—

it says

I should lose

ten pounds,

clean out my sewers,

comb my lawn,

learn jazz piano,

and spruce up

this rinky-dink operation—

Hey, rain,

can ya hear me?

I don't mind

being a recluse:

I'm not leaving

this porch—

Fern #3

I love
the fern's tips.

With fronds
like fur,

the lacy spears
follow

the sun.

When the weather
freezes,

the fern is
monstrous,

all arms
and legs:

yet it wants
to
live.

The Rain Has Lost Its Mind

The dying grass waits
    with its burnt tongue hanging out.

Rain begins to fall on the orange groves,
    fingers tapping hollow walls.

Suddenly, the rain loses its mind.

    Fireflies explode in the night.
    Elephants trample the clouds.

Wind tears away weakness:
here the aloe
    that soothes mosquito bites,
there the shed
    where birds nest
    in an old tool belt.

Electricity out.

Dog hides
    in the bathtub.

I'm just a wee creature.

I find oil lamps
and coax the dog
    into their light.

Catnip

(label on a jar on top of my refrigerator)

One spring my fiancé
set up our herb garden.
At first, he took it seriously.
We had parsley, sage, rosemary, and thyme,
just like Simon and Garfunkel,
and ginger, mint, dill, and catnip, besides.

But he didn't water,
didn't weed.
(He says he's not *a weeder.*)

It's hot here in Florida.
It's terrible hot.
He put up
this shade contraption,
wooden slats,
a kind of jail for herbs.

Soon they started falling down,
the slats.
And the herbs.

The thyme soon ran out of time.
Poor little dill
keeled over
like wilted asparagus stalks.
Rosemary and sage
never grew enough
to save.

My fiancé loved the mint.
Wanted to know
the recipe
for mint juleps.
And did we have
proper cups.

Sorry, I'm not up to polishing
my silver julep cups these days.
We'll use plastic.
Mint don't mind.
Mint's a weed.

All he had to do
was buy a ginger root
from the organic food store
and stick it in the ground.

His first ginger crop
tasted like horseradish.

He couldn't be
bothered
to stick
any more ginger roots
in the ground.

Goodbye, ginger.

Then it was goodbye, fiancé,

and I thought the herb garden
was finished
when the weeds took over.

But then there's catnip,
a hardy plant.

Catnip's a beacon.

One by one,
the feral cats in our rural neighborhood
strut around and around
the abandoned herb garden
on hot summer nights.

They perch
on a shade-slat amid the weeds
and begin
to yowl.

Spanish Moss

They're weighed down
with curly beards,

heavy ones
that itch and bind,

these grandpa trees

who can't breathe,

    and bits

    of beard
sail off each
      time

        the wind

            blows.

Mangos

Mangos smell rotten, and their meat is greasy on the tongue.

If a certain spider bites your finger when you're picking a bunch of bananas from the tree, you have to cut your finger off with a machete. Otherwise you die.

Mulberries are messy, dropping fruit on the ground, staining the lawn purple.

Strawberries get pecked by birds.

Loquat trees are fussy; they can't stand the cold.

Tomatoes gulp water like it's going out of style.

Forget peaches.

Key lime trees get some new disease every year. And they have thorns.

You, my child, have sensitive leaves and need constant watering. Once your roots take hold, however, you will bask in the sun and grow taller than this house.

Tomatoes

We had hundreds of green tomatoes,
    growing in pearly clusters like bells.

We thought as we bit into one:
    Colder than blood, but sweeter—

the first day of summer,
    clouds gathered in groups,

humidity fogged our eyeglasses,
    as mud swallowed the garden—

stealing their miniature hearts.

The Jogger

Lying in bed
is not an option,

although her doggy running partner
is gone now,

but her running shoes
don't give a darn:

her dog
has melted
into the tarry road,

the half-
awake
live oaks,

and the sound
of neighbor dogs'
barking.

Rain Again

Nothing's
more annoying

than the Florida rain.

Mothers
pat down
ruined hairdos.

Kids
skate
across Wal-Mart's floor.

Nothing's more fake
sincere
than the Florida rain,

slobbering,
licking houses,
leaving green mold
on concrete doorsteps,

goodbye letters
on clothes in the dryer,

dripping into attics
like sap.

It's always *there,*

the Florida rain,

hanging around,
like fingernails growing
when you're not looking,

seamless,
day in and day out,

the same soaked and muddy front lawn,
the same warm raindrops,

the same
supposedly soothing sounds,

although one morning,
I did witness
a heron
hurl
a burst of angry honks
into the deluge,

then fly
away.

Caterpillar

A caterpillar crossed
my sidewalk route,
green
as lime
Kool-Aid,
plump
as a balloon,

galumphing along
like a Chinese dragon,

segmented,
confident,

singing,
"DEE-dee-DEE-dee—."

And tennis shoes
sweat-lined,
neck
like a tree trunk,

I watched
as the green gate
of a garden
opened,

and
the caterpillar
crawled

through,

carefully
closing
the gate

after
itself.

The Orchid

How does she survive—
out in the cold,
roots naked?

Survive the rains
by combing her hair,

ruining it with an early sunset,
a razor
that erases, erases?

Geckos scamper
when disturbed,
but the orchid
won't budge,
stubbornly refusing
to die.

She keeps roots well-braced,
braiding them

with leaves
and seeds,

while her flowery future
sleeps in bare beds.

June

We cut weeds that choke the side fence
so snakes will vamoose,

when rain begins brushing the pines
like feathers tumbling, swishing.

Quick, you must pull your organic carrots—
No, too late for them—

The carrots whisper *tops* or *helpless*
as rain melts their sun-cooked flesh.

Thunder.
We read books in separate rooms.

I offer to look at your manuscript, the new one
where "father" comes to life.

First Semester at College

At dawn,
the yellow heat begins,

and our faces
harden and split
like coral.

We miss
the folks back home;

our thoughts tangled
like
yellow weeds.

We put on
our swim fins,

but swimming
isn't
an option.

And sometimes,
the yellow air
makes us feel faint,

but nights
we take our ease,

warm and wet
after soaking ourselves in the mud,

far from the pebbly beaches
where we grew up,

while the moon
tickles our fins

like
feathers
not yet invented.

The Office Dreams of Freedom

It's cold here and dusty; the air is perfectly still.
Voicemail sings when people are gone.
It pities the pencils locked in supply rooms.
It sings to its friends in offices everywhere.

Voicemail can sing when people are gone
Because it dreams that it's free to dream.
Voicemail makes friends in offices everywhere,
Meeting near fish tanks, lurking in halls.

Because it dreams, it's free to dream.
The phones fall silent when voicemail sings,
Meeting near fish tanks, lurking in halls,
As the office dreams of freedom.

The phones fall silent when voicemail sings
About the pencils locked in supply rooms.
When the office dreams of freedom,
It sings that it's cold here and dusty
And the air is perfectly still.

The Philosopher

When he talks,
a group gathers.

Does life have any meaning?

His steak cools,
his child coos,
his dreadlocks flow.

Peeling a grape,
he leans down to his wife:

Is anything real?

Goldfish Soap Opera

Yesterday
Mama fish bit Leroy
between his head and his gills
on his belly side.

They are both big fish,
big as dinner entrees.

Leroy has
a pencil eraser-sized
puncture wound,
red flesh
bulging out
like a hernia.

Mama,
orange scales
covering her blush,
lies low against the gravel,
shame in her eyes.

But they both
live on.

Antibiotics
and
Poseidon

saved them.

After Me, Annihilation

—Remark attributed to Louis XVI, implying he didn't care about consequences since he'd be dead.

When I heard about
the next world war,
I stuck a stone in my backpack, a stolen star.

I had to unplug
my electric sheep.
I wore pink lipstick; I paid to cheat.

I baked in a bunker,
buried in my dress,
as hot birds flew bombs north by northwest.

I walked crooked streets
in my high heels.
I saw no other people for ten thousand miles.

I slept with an old sock.
I ate a moral pear.
In a dark car, I was washing my hair

in ashes and Dove
when a 'bot knocked on the door
and said, *Have you heard? We finally won the war.*

Raven

(Birds, Frogs, & Clouds Cento #2*)

Raven would

fly in circles over land and sea,

the sound of wings

beating

and twirling.

She smelled of perfume,

saffron,

smoke-filled flames

in a circular box.

She was

a woman

who could

at the same time be

both old and young.

Translator: Ian Johnson

The Stargazer

He owns
a gimongous telescope,
and a cell phone app

tells him exactly
where
all the stars and planets
are located.

His screensaver
is
a galaxy.

He travels
thousands of miles

to see eclipses
through funny glasses,

but he never looks down
to see

the earth

under his own
flip-flopped feet.

Who Can Tell When She's Awake?

Can anyone sleep
this steamy summer night?
Not me.
I'm in bed,
imagining

I'm in a space station
a million miles from Mars,
with only an intelligent computer
to share
my secrets with.

I shift my mass
on the mattress,
my sorry spaceship,
my heavy, mortal body.

No stars
out the window;
overcast skies
blanket me.
It's so hot
my ship can't take off.

Too bad,
because I carry
a full load of alien goods,
including a pill
guaranteed

to transport
the person
who swallows it

to
somewhere else.

What I Remember

The winding staircase of our love,

The battered boxes of our hearts,

The collapsing bed of our fights,

The skylights of our sleep.

The Color of Waiting

A paint swatch on paper

is more compelling

than a number—

we don't know how long

the bursting

will take.

Tulips

in the ground

will first

send up shoots,

and soon the shoots have fits,

getting ready

to bloom.

But tulips in pots

on the porch

take their sweet time,

days flowing

like eggs

dipped in weak blue dye,

an odd yearning,

waiting in water

and earth

and cold.

The Longest Night

Well, we made it
through the longest night
of the year,

and we earned it—

the happiness

of daylight—

we waited and waited

and the moon is strange
when clouds
are clumpy

and when rooms
aren't empty,

but dense with darkness—

but now, the sun
kicks in—

stronger and stronger
each day,

like a sick man
recovering from the flu:

a little bit grumpy,

but still glad to see you.

Ants

You came home late, sweaty, dressed in your uniform, carrying your duffle bag, and I told you I'd gotten rid of the hundreds of ants that were swarming over the fat in your breakfast frying pan that you'd left on the stove. You responded that I didn't appreciate all you did for me, paying half the expenses, taking out the garbage, and mowing the lawn.

Then *I* said that I hadn't signed a contract to be a Stepford Wife, so why did I have to scrub your greasy pans? And that the ants were crawling over me by the time I finished, and I had to spray Clorox on the them like an ethnic cleansing—

and you yelled that I was trying to poison us all—

and as we continued to argue, out of the corner of my eye I saw an army of ants sneaking into the kitchen from a crack under the window,

darkening
      the kitchen
           counters
               in

                  a

                     gradually

                       swelling

                          line.

Beef Tips

I love to stick my hand
in my dog's mouth–

good practice to train him to be gentle,
or so I tell my husband, who looks at me like I'm *loca*–

with dripping left-over beef tips and gravy from
Publix
on my fingertips–

and, his black Lab teeth
barely clipping me,

he licks me clean
with his greedy *carpe diem* tongue.

Dog Haiku

Day-and-night hot rain
Gifts us with minutes of sun:
Dogs roll in the mud.

In the garden by
The house, dogs chase frogs. Surprise—
Frogs leap out of range.

Fog at four a.m.
When I let the three dogs out,
They turn into ghosts.

The High Diver

When it's your turn,
you must not
hesitate.

No holding back.

No
long pauses,

toes hanging over the end of the board,

staring
at the water
far below.

Deep breath,
look,
go.

A loud burst
when you cut the water,
but underneath,
all sounds are cotton,

and light is
blue-and-white
with odd wavelengths.

No one
swims

in the deep end
for long.

You climb out of the pool:

a suctioning sound
as your feet scrape
the wrinkled deck.

Your nose
is sunburned,
hair wet and dribbling.

People lounging on deck chairs,
sipping cocktails
and fanning themselves,

don't say a word
about your dive.

They are eying
the next diver now.

Meanwhile, you
circle back
and return to the line.

T'ang

Can a horse be sarcastic?

A terra cotta two-foot-high replica of a Chinese
T'ang Dynasty horse prances at the center of my
dining room table. I call him T'ang after his era.
He's obviously a show-horse: three of his hooves are
grounded, attached to the base, but his right front
hoof is lifted coyly, as if he's saying, *Am I not gorgeous?*

T'ang's ears thrust straight up. Wearing a show saddle,
he carries his docked tail high. His grin is huge,
almost manic; his top and bottom teeth are like bricks.

I have to carefully arrange T'ang on the table so he
faces the room and isn't showing his plump rear end
to anything or anyone except the wall. The round
wooden table is shiny, and he has a habit of sliding on
it when I'm not looking. He'd dance around the house
like crazy if I let him loose.

But when he doesn't behave, I herd him back into his
stall under the sink. He laughs at me and I slam the
cabinet door.

Spring Haiku

I'm walking the dogs
In the tall grass across the street,
Watching the sunset.

A black racer snake
Like a sleek licorice whip
Chases a gecko.

Poor little gecko
Loses part of his long tail.
But it will grow back.

A toad likes to lurk
By the front door near my boots.
Next, he'll hide in them.

Strawberries and cake,
Vanilla ice cream on top,
Dripping with red juice.

Time to go to bed.
One last dog walk, one last look
At the stars above.

Full moon competes with
Clouds pouring past its pale face
In the silent sky.

Gestural Shape of a Woman

Rain pelting the window
as a woman dreams

is like thrown gravel
or bullets.

A cobra strikes.

Boiling water molecules bump together
in a copper teapot.

Flashbulbs leap into eyes,
leaving
a burning trail.

A Venus-flytrap grabs its dinner.

In her dream,
she is robed,

and she
pluck,
pluck,
plucks

her harp.

The Fairy Tale Princess

Surrounded by puffs of gauzy gown,

waving at commoners from her coach,

simpering under her tiara,

protected by her trusty guards,

attended by her lusty maids,

nibbling petite portions from gilded plates
at gala dinners,

sitting to have her portrait painted,

getting fitted for new dresses:

the princess
waits

(and waits and waits)

for
her prince.

Cheating

I was long on the crossword puzzle,
      then on two pillows
           in bed on Sunday
               afternoon,
when in my July sleep,
      vibration and gurgle
           like someone pulled the plug
               on a giant bath
                  tub.
Must be thunder and I am on my side and then
thunder.
      Legs are bent
           and mild eyes goodnighting.
               I'm home
from treadmill and yoga
      with my sister who's lost one hundred pounds,
        and stretching hurts no matter how careful I
am
                  to baby
the shoulder where the January operation
      still smolders, and I ask myself which meds
           on today's menu

sack me so sleepy and so far and
then

thunder.

The Tattooed Man

His right shoulder says
don't worry be happy
and symbols for infinity

and musical notes
are sprinkled up and down
his right arm.

On his left arm,
Cry havoc & let slip the hounds of war.

He got that in Iraq.

He drums lightly on his dog's ribs,
making a hollow sound.

The dog loves it.

The Florida Anoles

The anoles
      in the azalea bushes wind around
            branches like wavy hair:
hundreds of anoles
      hiding Escher-like
            in chain link fences,
under palmetto bushes, on concrete
      block walks, under the mist
            hovering over the vacant lot
next door like fabric softener sheets.
      They are ribbons
            tying me to these orchids
on this front porch
      in the town
            of my childhood.
I have returned,
      they have tasted me,
            and I taste like their own blood.

Going

The butterflies have left your eyes,
The warmth of your body fades into stars,
Your sharp needle and my dark loom,
Lives we've been weaving since we were born.

The warmth of your body fades into stars.
You cartwheel away because you are fleeing
The lives we've been weaving since we were born.
The day we've been dreaming has finally arrived.

When you cartwheel away because you are fleeing
Beyond all the threads that I can control,
The day we've been dreaming has finally arrived
Amid lullaby hospital sounds.

Beyond all the threads that I can control,
The butterflies have left your eyes
Amid lullaby hospital sounds:
Your sharp needle and my dark loom.

Nocturne
—*after Eric Satie, "Gymnopedie No. 2"*

My baby brother's
footsteps
are
rain
on the roof tonight.

Piano chords
reach towards me
like arms.

After the storm,
a humid mist
descends.

Feathers trail
from
the full
yellow moon,

soon
disappearing.

I Wish

Grandma,
I wish
we could sit down
at your Formica table
in your kitchen in Tampa

and eat grapes
and drink Cokes from the bottle
to keep cool.

You always slipped me
a few bucks
because you knew
money escaped me,

but you didn't mind
the way I was.

I wish I could take you shopping.
I'd buy you
a pair of red shoes.

You always liked shoes.

I wish I could
wrap you
into a piece of bread
and carry you in my purse

and when I needed you,
I'd pull off a piece

and let you
dissolve
on my tongue.

Eileen "Mish" Murphy lives near Tampa with her Chi-Spaniel Cookie. She teaches English and literature at Polk State College. Her poems have been published in numerous journals, including *Tinderbox Journal, Rogue Agent,* and *Thirteen Myna Birds.* She is a staff writer for *Cultural Weekly.* A prolific book reviewer and visual artist, she has also done the illustrations for the highly acclaimed children's book *Phoebe and Ito are dogs* written by John Yamrus. *Fortune Written on Wet Grass* is her first full length collection.

Acknowledgements

"After Me, Annihilation." *George & Mertie's Place,* 2000. Reprinted in *Post Amerikan No. 6,* 2000-2001, in *Poets Against the War* [Anthology], Sam Hamill, Editor, Thunder Mouth Press, 2003, and in *Autumn Sky Daily,* 2017.

"Beef Tips." *Obsession Literary Magazine,* 2013. Reprinted in *Writing In A Woman's Voice,* 2018.

"Caterpillar." *KotaPress,* 2003.

"Cheating." *poetry/memoir/story,* 2004. Reprinted in *Pittsburgh Poetry Houses,* 2016, and in *Rag Queen Periodical,* 2018.

"The Color of Waiting." *Uppagus,* 2016.

"The Florida Anoles." *Writing In A Woman's Voice,* 2018.

"Gestural Shape of a Woman." *Emergence III,* 1996.

"Going." *Thirteen Myna Birds,* 2019.

"The High Diver." *Sandhill Review,* 2016.

"I Wish." *KotaPress,* 2003. Reprinted in *Autumn Sky Daily,* 2018.

"June." *Right Hand Pointing Issue 94,* 2016.

"Nocturne." *Writing In A Woman's Voice,* 2018.

"The Office Dreams of Freedom." *Autumn Sky Daily,* 2016.

"The Philosopher." *Straight Forward,* 2015.

"The Rain Has Lost Its Mind." *The Open Mouse,* 2017.

"The Tattooed Man." *The Open Mouse,* 2017.

"What I Remember." *Thirteen Myna Birds,* 2019.

Thank you to the Wapshott Press sponsors, supporters, and Friends of the Wapshott Press.

Muna Deriane
Kit Ramage
Rachel Livingston
Kathleen Warner
Ann and John Brantingham
Marilyn Robertson
Suzanne Siegel
Toni Rodriguez
James and Rebecca White
Leslie Bohem
David Meischen
James Wilson
Robert Earle and Mary Azoy
Kathleen Bonagofsky
Phil Temples
Richard Whittaker
Ann Siemens
Elaine Padilla
Laurel Sutton
John Grigor Bell

The Wapshott Press is a 501(c)(3) not-for-profit enterprise publishing work by emerging and established authors and artists. We publish books that should be published. We are very grateful to the people who believe in our plans and goals, as well as our hopes and dreams. Our new website is at www.WapshottPress. org. Donations gratefully accepted at www.Donate. WapshottPress.org.

www.ingramcontent.com/pod-product-compliance
Lightning Source LLC
Chambersburg PA
CBHW071213130626
46555CB00004B/1693